Be Your Type of Super Rising Purpose Peep Activities To Find The Hero In You

By Dena Wiggins, MBA, CPC

ISBN: 978-0-9986708-9-8

Dedicated To Rising Purpose Peeps
On Your Journey To
Unlock The Hero Or Heroine In You! I See You.
I Believe In You! You've Got This!

BE
Verb
1. Exist
2. Occur, Take Place

YOUR
Determiner
Belonging To Or Associated With The
Person Or People The Speaker Is Addressing

TYPE OF
Noun
a person or thing symbolizing or exemplifying
the ideal or defining characteristics of
something

SUPER
Combining Form Prefix
1. Above, Over, Beyond
2. To A Great Degree

Be

Isn't About Doing A
Bunch of Stuff But Being
YOU

Your

This Is About You
Discovering Your Answers

Type Of

This Is About You Understanding
Your Uniqueness

Super

That Will Help You Unlock What
Comes After The Prefix Super

To Complete These Exercises Requires:
✔ Your Open Mind
✔ Honesty With Yourself
✔ Being OK With Not Having All Of The Answers
✔ Sticking With It Until The End
✔ Open To Believing Your Life Has Meaning Just Because YOU Exist
✔ Open To Believing That You Have A Super That Gives Your Life MORE Meaning

_____

Signature   Date
This Is Your Promise To Yourself

Think of one of your favorite movies. In the beginning of the movie, you see the main character being, "normal." As the story continues, you see the plot or type of journey he or she is on and the different things he or she must overcome to triumph over the main problem. This is also called the Hero's or Heroine's Journey. During the steps of the journey, the main character's type of super is revealed!

1 2 3 4 5 6 7 8

If you watched a movie of your life called
Being

_____

(your name)
describe what you see, knowing the characters & scenes as a part of what's happening

What Is Your Ordinary Life?

"Heroes and Heroines Are Ordinary People Who Do *EXTRA*ordinary Things Through His or Her Type of *SUPER.*"

This journey is about understanding the way that *YOU* help people in the SUPER way that turns your *ORDINARY WORLD* into *SUPER* possibilities for yourself and others. To do this let's unlock

The Hero's / Heroine's Journey.

Created By Joseph Campbell, The Hero's Journey is adapted from his book, *The Hero With A Thousand Faces.* It describes the phases of hero development that is the basis of Greek mythology and modern storytelling *including your emerging story!*

The Hero's Or Heroine's Journey Unlocked

The hero or heroine is living in the ordinary world. The ordinary world is the day-to-day routine or norm of the hero or heroine.	**1** **The Ordinary World**
The Call To Adventure **2**	This is the event that begins the journey. This event shakes up the normal, ordinary routine. Sometimes the change is welcomed by the hero or heroine. Most of the time, the call comes as an unexpected challenge or problem.
This is the *in between* step when the hero or heroine hesitates, questions, or weighs the cost of the call before accepting the call and moving forward.	**3** **The Refusal of the Call**
Meets The Mentor **4**	The hero or heroine meets with a mentor who guides them. The mentor provides wisdom for the steps ahead. The age of the mentor does not matter.
The hero or heroine commits the adventure knowing it is different but not fully knowing what to expect.	**5** **Crossing The First Threshold**
Tests, Allies & Enemies **6**	Allies show up and partner with the hero or heroine. The protagonist is also revealed.
The hero of heroine comes to the center of the journey and is met with tests that reveal the treasure of the story .	**7** **Approach To The Innermost Cave**
The Ordeal **8**	The hero or heroine is pushed to give up completely. This is when the person who began the journey transforms to the hero or heroine. Before this happens, the hero or heroine feels they must give up.

What Are Your Thoughts?

The Hero's Or Heroine's Journey
Wizard of Oz Example

Dorothy is the heroine. We see her in her everyday life in Kansas. Dorothy is bored and sings Somewhere Over The Rainbow as she longs for adventure.	**The Ordinary World** 1
The Call To Adventure 2	Dorothy's journey begins when she decides to save her dog during a tornado. She awakes from being unconscious and is in a new world unlike anything she has ever seen.
Dorothy downplays the reality that her home lands on an evil witch freeing the people of the land from land.	3 **The Refusal of the Call**
Meets The Mentor 4	Glenda, The Good Witch, is Dorothy's mentor who guides her to the yellow brick road to the Wizard of Oz. Glenda also gifts Dorothy with the ruby slippers.
Dorothy follows The yellow brick road with only her dog, Todo & her ruby slippers.	5 **Crossing The First Threshold**
Tests, Allies & Enemies 6	Dorothy meets three allies on the yellow brick road who share the goal of meeting the Wizard of Oz to fulfill a goal. The team are tested along the way by the new nemesis, The Wicked Witch of the West.
Dorothy travels to the home of the Evil Witch to retrieve her broom for the Wizard of Oz to help her, Scarecrow, Tin Man and Lion.	7 **Approach To The Innermost Cave**
The Ordeal 8	Dorothy's allies are captured, and she faces certain demise at the hands of the Evil Witch. Dorothy douses the Evil Witch with water which melts her. The people are freed & she has the broom to exchange with the Wizard of Oz.

Dorothy returns home while reciting there is no place like home and realizing the truth that being home surrounded by family is better than over the rainbow.

What Do You See?

The Hero's Or Heroine's Journey
Harry Potter

Harry Potter is living an invisible life as an orphan, living under the stairs of the home of his Aunt & Uncle.	**1** **The Ordinary World**
The Call To Adventure **2**	Harry receives the magical invitation to Hogwarts.
Harry doubts that he should accept. He does not believe he has what it takes. Harry accepts when he feels he can no longer stay with his relatives.	**3** **The Refusal of the Call**
Meets The Mentor **4**	Professor Dumbledore, headmaster at Hogwarts becomes Harry's mentor. He guides Harry knowing more about his true role and history at Hogwarts.
Harry learns the truth about how he died.	**5** **Crossing The First Threshold**
Tests, Allies & Enemies **6**	Harry has many tests to overcome to discover and defeat his enemy Voldemort. Harry also befriends fierce allies in Hagrid, Ron and Hermione.
Harry, Ron and Hermione travel through many secret caves to get to the layer that holds the Sorcerer's Stone.	**7** **Approach To The Innermost Cave**
The Ordeal **8**	Harry discovers one of his professors is really his nemesis, Voldemort, and a huge battle ensues. Harry awakens recovering from his injuries to learn his mother's love protected him from Voldemort.
Harry returns to the ordinary world knowing he is extraordinary, deeply loved and commited to return to Hogwartz next term.	

What Did You See?

The Hero's Or Heroine's Journey
Mulan Example

Mulan is living her ordinary life and experiencing her cultural traditions for being a woman and bringing honor to her family.	**1** **The Ordinary World**
The Call To Adventure **2**	The empire is threatened by the Huns. Men are drafted to the army including Mulan's father. Given the health and age of her father, Mulan is against this. Something shifts for Mulan when she sees her frail father wielding his sword.
Mulan is conflicted by her love of her family, love for her country and respect for tradition and honor. She decides to do something unheard of when the cost of doing nothing could be the death of her father.	**3** **The Refusal of the Call**
Meets The Mentor **4**	Mushu becomes an unlikely mentor to Mulan after causing a mishap to connect with the *likely* mentor for Mulan.
With the help of Mushu, Mulan successfully infiltrates the army posing as a male soldier, Ping.	**5** **Crossing The First Threshold**
Tests, Allies & Enemies **6**	Although Mulan is awkward in her disguise, she eventually befriends soldiers, Yao, Ling and Chien-Po. Her resolve impresses the army captain. Hun's army is approaching.
Hun's army ambushes Mulan's troop. Mulan uses a canon to start an avalanche burying a lot of the Huns. Mulan is injured by the leader of the Huns.	**7** **Approach To The Innermost Cave**
The Ordeal **8**	When Mulan's wound is bandaged, her deception is discovered. Instead of facing death, her captain spared her life and expelled her from the army. Mulan realizes the leader of the Huns lived and is returning. No one believes her.

Mulan returns home a warrior with great skill in strategy. With the help of her allies, the empire is saved from the Huns and Mulan's family is honored for her bravery.

How Did You See Things?

The Hero's Or Heroine's Journey
Black Panther Example

T'Challa is living a life of comfort in Wakanda, which looks like a third world country to others. His country possesses vibranium, which is transformed into sophisticated modern technologies.	**The Ordinary World** ①
The Call To Adventure ②	T'Challa's father, T'Chaka, is killed and T'Challa is to be crowned king of Wakanda.
T'Challa does not believe he is ready. He questions his ability to lead like his father. He meets with his father in the spirit realm and is assured. He awkwardly defends his crown against a challenger for the throne persuading him to yield rather than die.	**The Refusal of the Call** ③
Meets The Mentor ④	T'Challa's mentors are his father, whom he meets in the spirit realm after ingesting vibranium. His earthly mentor is his father's best friend, Zuri.
Shortly after T'Challa is Crowned King, his first mission is the bring back Klaue, who stole Wakandan artifacts and threatens the secrecy and safety of the country.	**Crossing The First Threshold** ⑤
Tests, Allies & Enemies ⑥	T'Challa's allies that help him are his sister, Shuri his past love, Nakia, Ross from the new world, the leader of his army Okoye. He also meets his cousin, Erik Killmonger, who is a fierce enemy.
T'Challa discovers his father is responsible for the death of his uncle and the abandonment of his cousin to hide to hide the truth.	**Approach To The Innermost Cave** ⑦
The Ordeal ⑧	Erik returns to Wakanda and defeats T'Challa for the throne. T'Challa is severely wounded and thought dead. He is rescued in retribution for his kindness and returns with his allies to defeat Erik.

T'Challa returns to Wakanda changed and determined to lead Wakanda to a future of sharing its technology with the new world in honor of Erik's view of empowering people in the new world.

What Would You Change?

The Hero's Or Heroine's Journey
Can You Imagine The Journey Of a Friend?

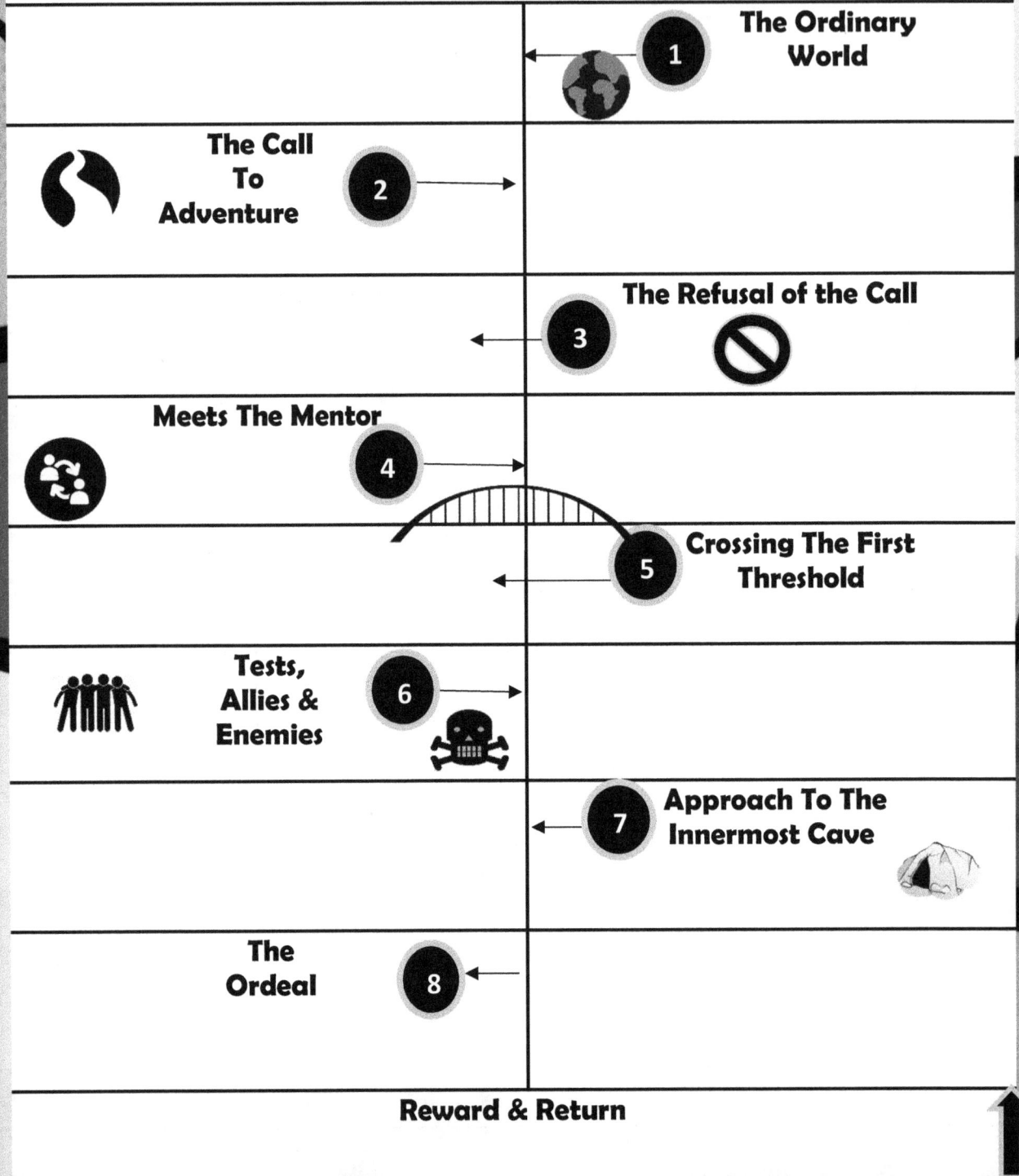

	1 **The Ordinary World**
The Call To Adventure **2** →	
	3 ← **The Refusal of the Call**
Meets The Mentor **4** →	
	5 **Crossing The First Threshold**
Tests, Allies & Enemies **6** →	
	7 ← **Approach To The Innermost Cave**
The Ordeal **8** ←	
Reward & Return	

What Surprised You?

Do You Recognize Any Of The Characters?

The Hero's Or Heroine's Journey

Can You Imagine The Journey Of A Family Member?

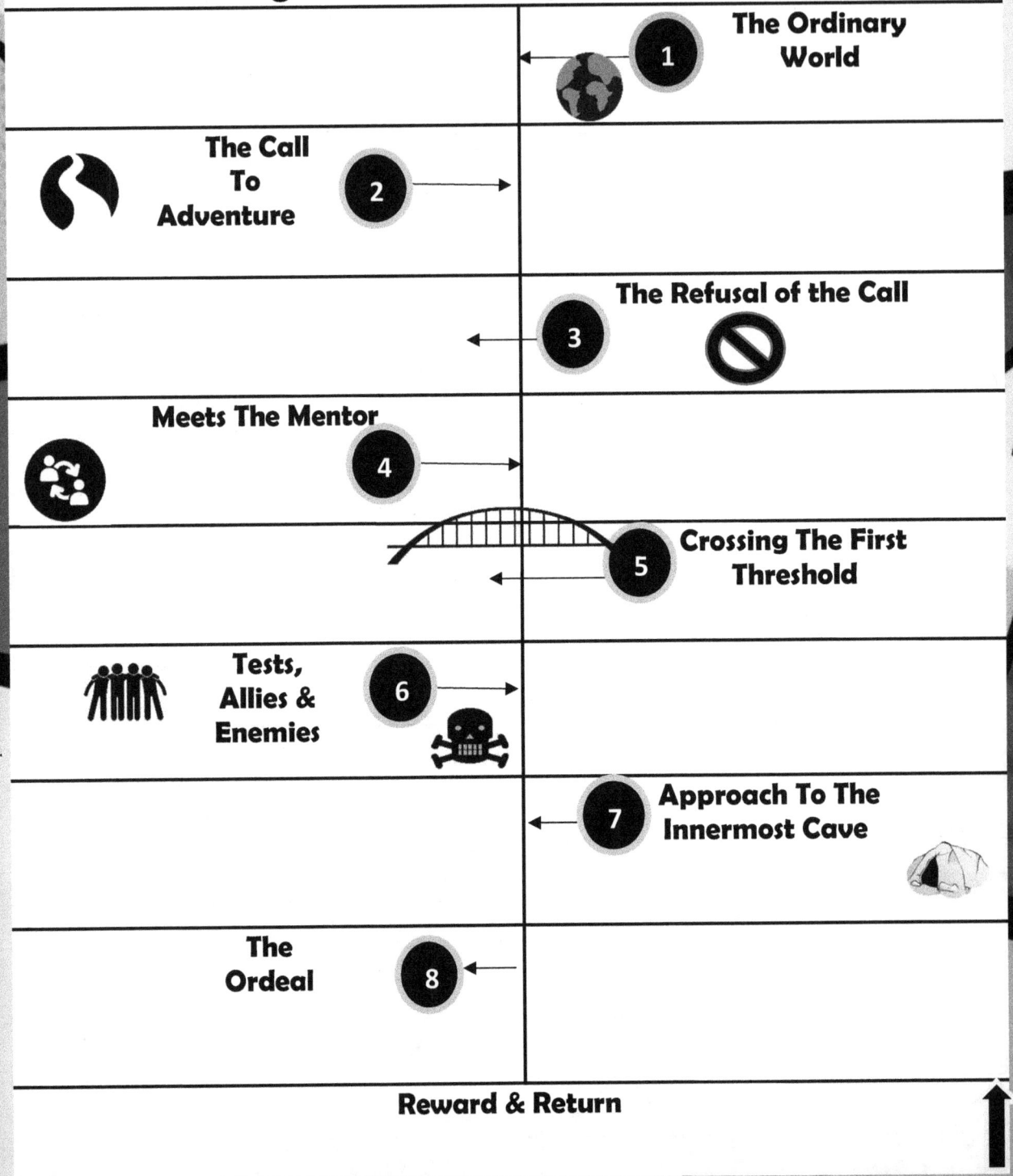

	The Ordinary World 1
The Call To Adventure 2	
	The Refusal of the Call 3
Meets The Mentor 4	
	5 **Crossing The First Threshold**
Tests, Allies & Enemies 6	
	7 **Approach To The Innermost Cave**
The Ordeal 8	
Reward & Return	

What Did You Learn?

The Hero's Or Heroine's Journey

Can You Interview A Mentor?

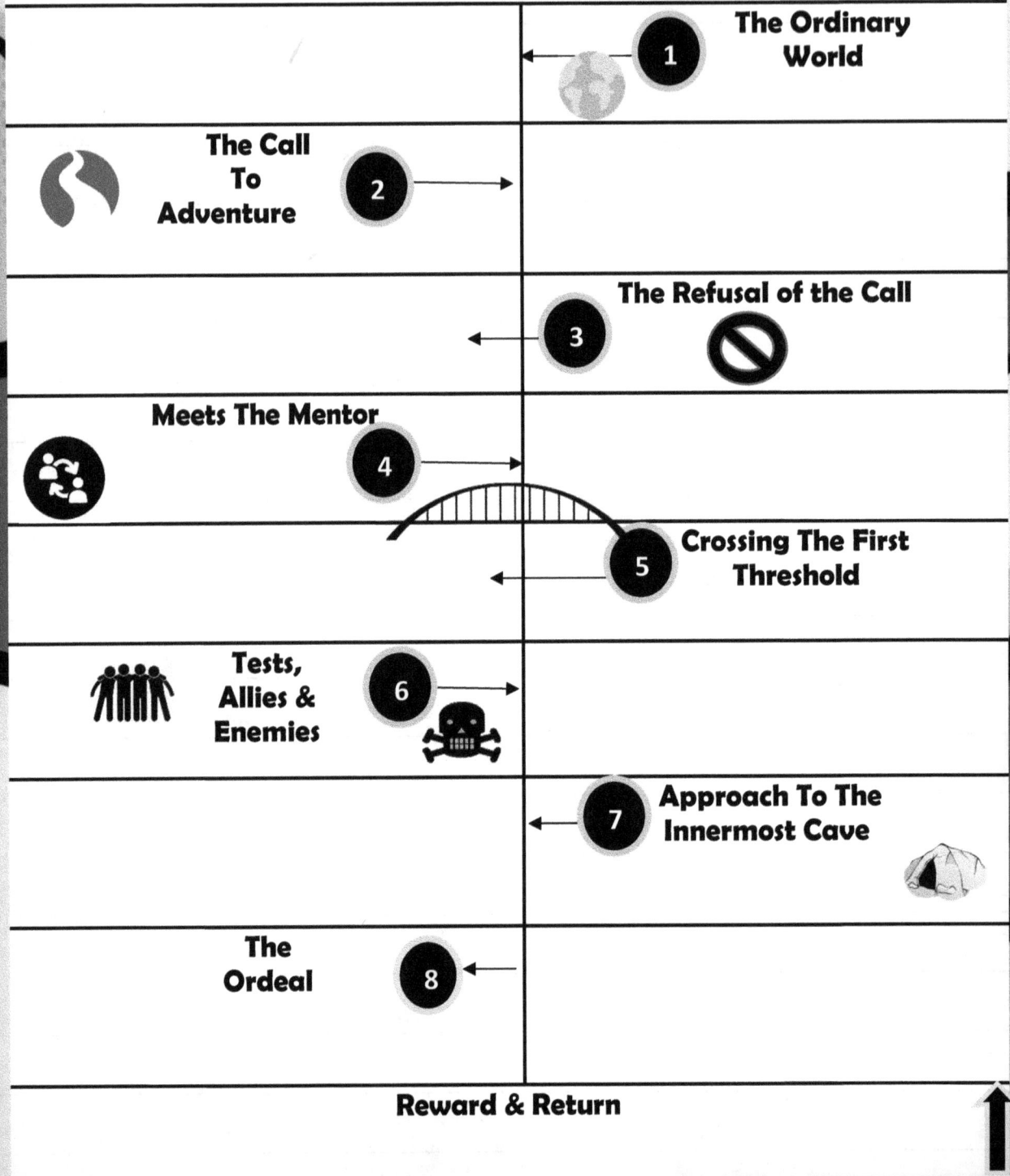

	1 The Ordinary World
The Call To Adventure **2**	
	3 The Refusal of the Call
Meets The Mentor **4**	
	5 Crossing The First Threshold
Tests, Allies & Enemies **6**	
	7 Approach To The Innermost Cave
The Ordeal **8**	
Reward & Return	

What Did You Learn?

The Hero's Or Heroine's Journey
What About YOUR Journey?

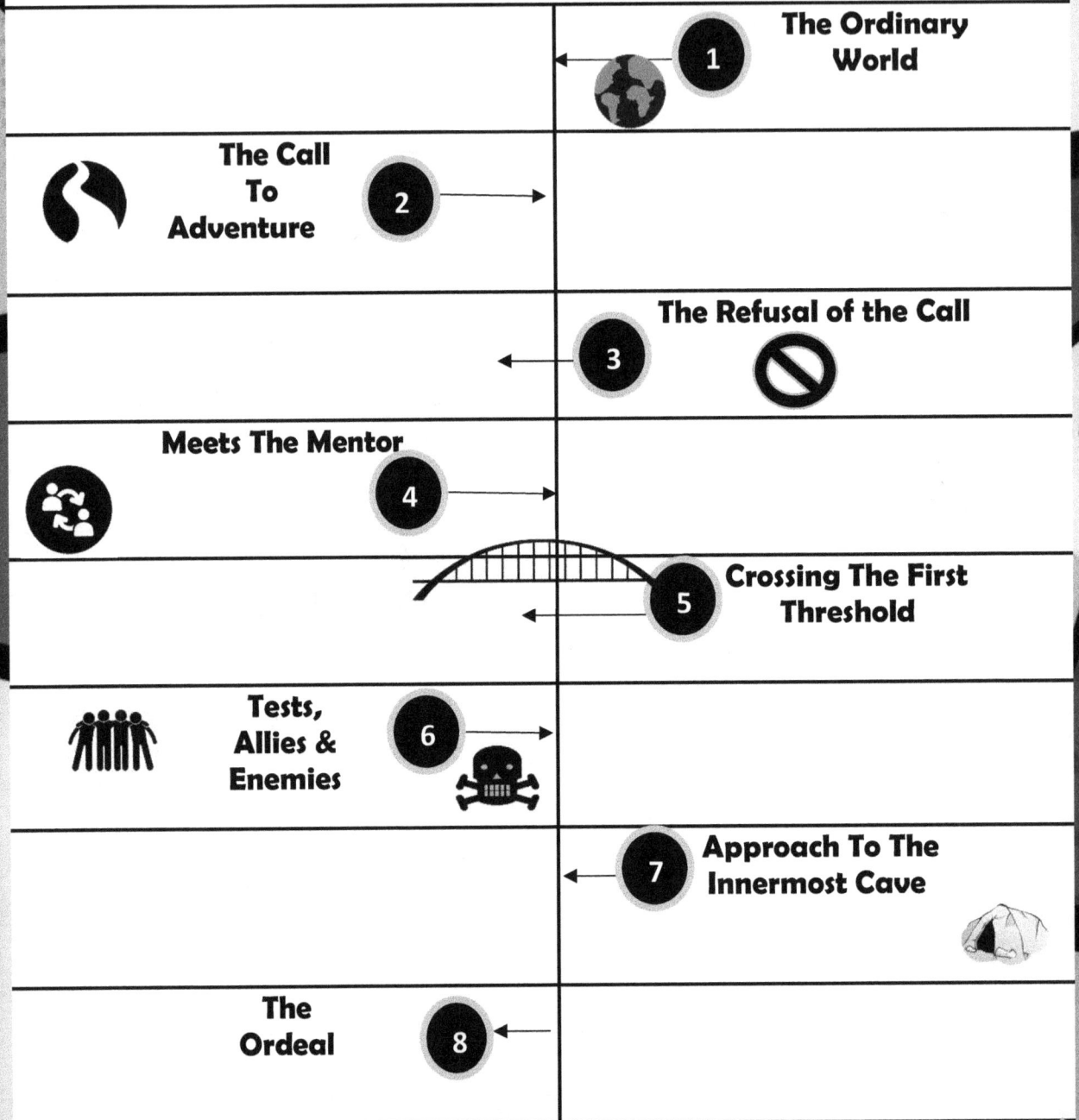

	The Ordinary World ← 1
The Call To Adventure 2 →	
	The Refusal of the Call ← 3
Meets The Mentor 4 →	
	Crossing The First Threshold ← 5
Tests, Allies & Enemies 6 →	
	Approach To The Innermost Cave ← 7
The Ordeal 8 ←	

Reward & Return ↑

"It's NORMAL to not know all of the answers and to fill in all the blanks. START with what you know... Come back and fill in as you KNOW MORE & GROW."

What Did You Learn?

Who Are Your Mentors & What Did They Teach You?

Who Are Your Allies?

Observations About
The Hero's / Heroine's Journey

1 HEROS/HEROINES
are everyday people who learn
they are super at or about
something actionable,
a character trait
or quality

2 REAL LIFE TAKES
more than 3 hours to tell a
story like a movie! Some
journeys take months,
years or several times
coming to the same
step before going
further

3 THE JOURNEY
is also called the path to purpose.
It is a journey to understand
who you are and how
who you are
helps
others

4 EVERYONE HAS
stuff to overcome. Everyone
has ordeals, people that are
for and against them and
times they want to quit
just before the
BREAK
through

5 EVERYTIME
cHAnGe happens, there is an
adjustment & the question is
how much and how long
it will take to get
used to
it

6 WE ALL NEED
help sometimes from both
friends who believe in us
and show up for us &
from mentors who
share wisdom &
guide us along
the way

**Just when you think you've gotten used to change,
there will come a new call to adventure that
begins another journey. Have you noticed
that a lot of movies have sequels
after it seems the story is complete?**

Observations About
The Hero's / Heroine's Journey

RELATIONSHIPS MATTER
- ✓ Mentors Believe You Can Do It
- ✓ Friends Journey With You & Will Help You
- ✓ Focus On Friends & What Is Good In Your Life During Times of Trouble
- ✓ People & Things That Come Against You Have A Purpose— They Push You Toward Your Super If You Do Not Give UP!

IMPACT
- ✓ Every Journey Starts In The Ordinary World
- ✓ Calls To Adventure Can Move You Out of The Ordinary World Also Called Comfort Zone
- ✓ You Have The Choice To Accept The Call
- ✓ Trials, Tests & Challenges May Make You Feel Like Quitting Just Before *YOUR* Super Is Revealed That Gets You To A Breakthrough

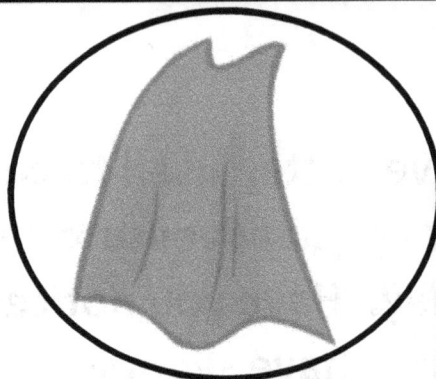

GROWTH
- ✓ You Grow Into Your Super Throughout Your Hero Or Heroine Journey
- ✓ The Things You Learn Are For You During Your Journey & To Take Back To The Ordinary World
- ✓ Being Super In The Ordinary World Requires Practice So You Don't Forget Your Super

The Hero's / Heroine's Journey
Relationship Reflection

Who Are Your Mentors That Believe You Can Do It?

Who Are Your Allies That Share Your Goals & Direction?

Who Are Your Friends, Your Tribe That Are There In Good Times & Bad Times?

The Hero's / Heroine's Journey
Impact Reflection

What Moves You Out of Your Ordinary World (Comfort Zone)?

What Are You Really Passionate About?

Who Receives The Gifts You Take Back To The Ordinary World?

The Hero's / Heroine's Journey
Growth Reflection

What Changed From The Beginning of Your Journey To Now?

What skills or knowledge are you building?

Who Supports How You Are Growing & Changing?

"SPEND time BEING in the moment & every once in a while, CHECK IN & REVIEW your life like watching a movie. It's hard to notice things when you're busy living."

The Hero's Or Heroine's Journey

End of 6th Grade Reflection

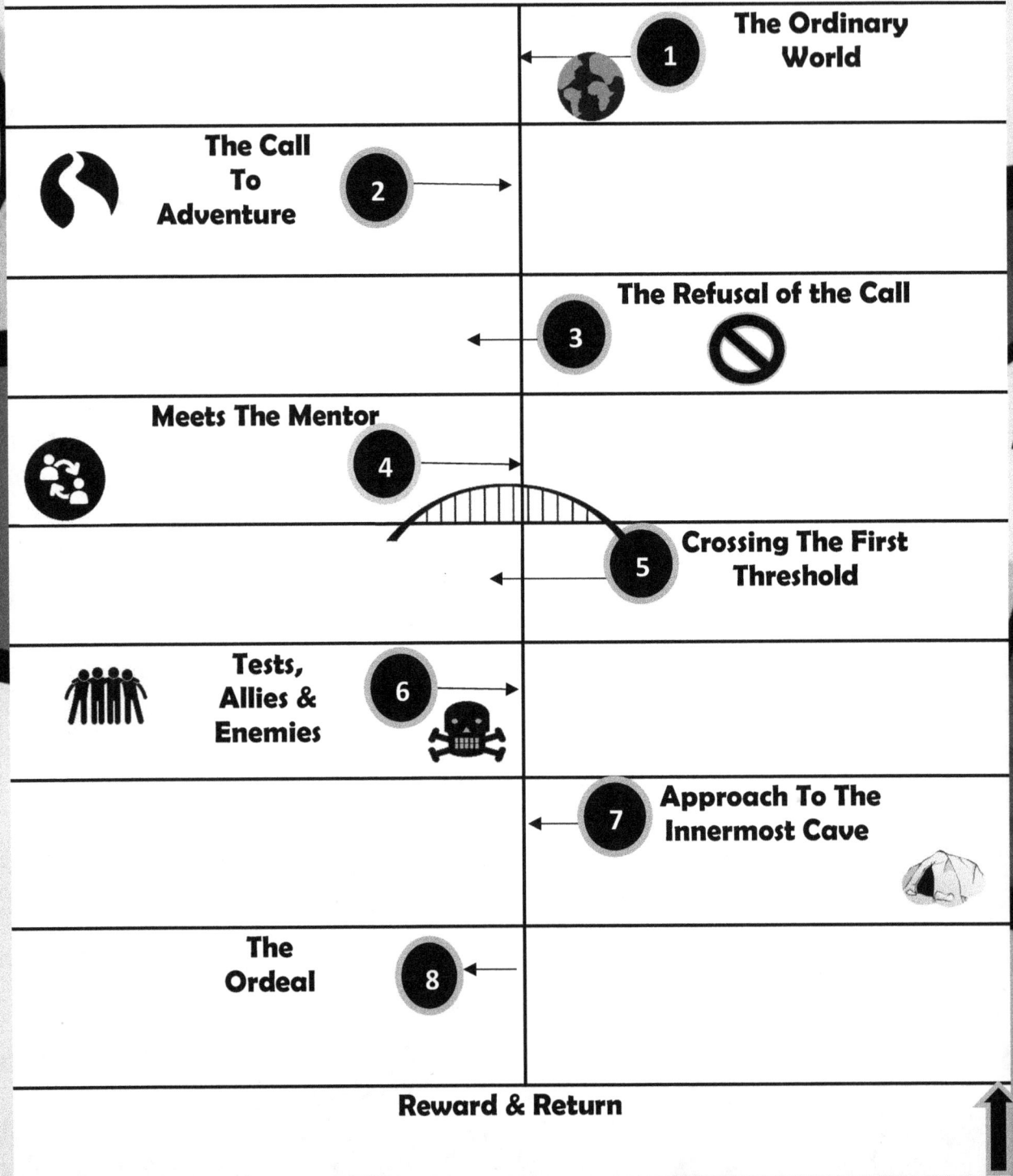

	The Ordinary World — 1
The Call To Adventure — 2	
	3 — **The Refusal of the Call**
Meets The Mentor — 4	
	5 — **Crossing The First Threshold**
Tests, Allies & Enemies — 6	
	7 — **Approach To The Innermost Cave**
The Ordeal — 8	

Reward & Return

What Do You See?
What Rewards Can You Take With You To The Next Year?

The Hero's Or Heroine's Journey
End of 7th Grade Reflection

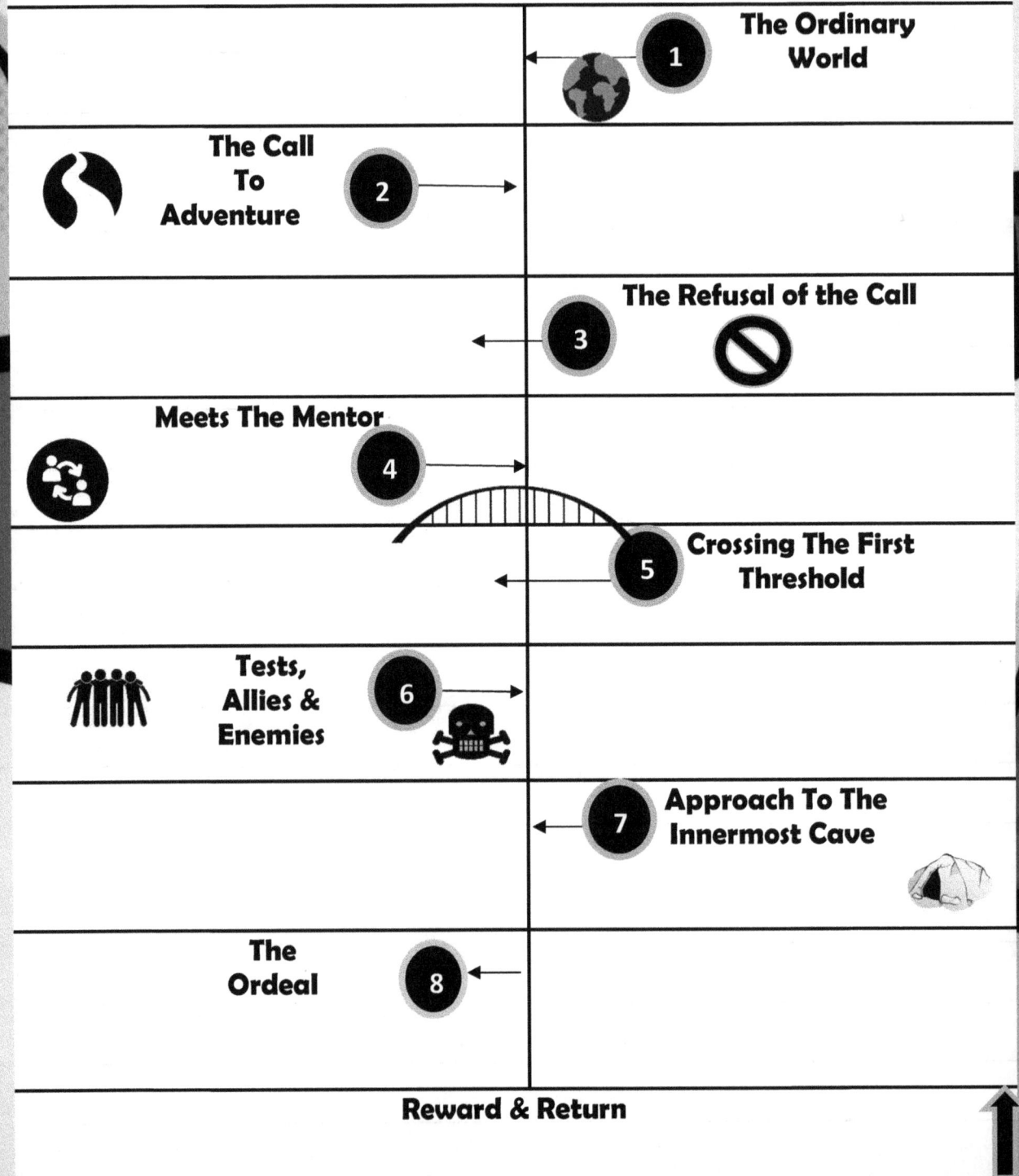

	The Ordinary World ← 1
The Call To Adventure 2 →	
	The Refusal of the Call ← 3
Meets The Mentor 4 →	
	Crossing The First Threshold ← 5
Tests, Allies & Enemies 6 →	
	Approach To The Innermost Cave ← 7
The Ordeal 8 ←	
Reward & Return	

What Do You See?
What Rewards Can You Take With You To The Next Year?

The Hero's Or Heroine's Journey

End of 8th Grade Reflection

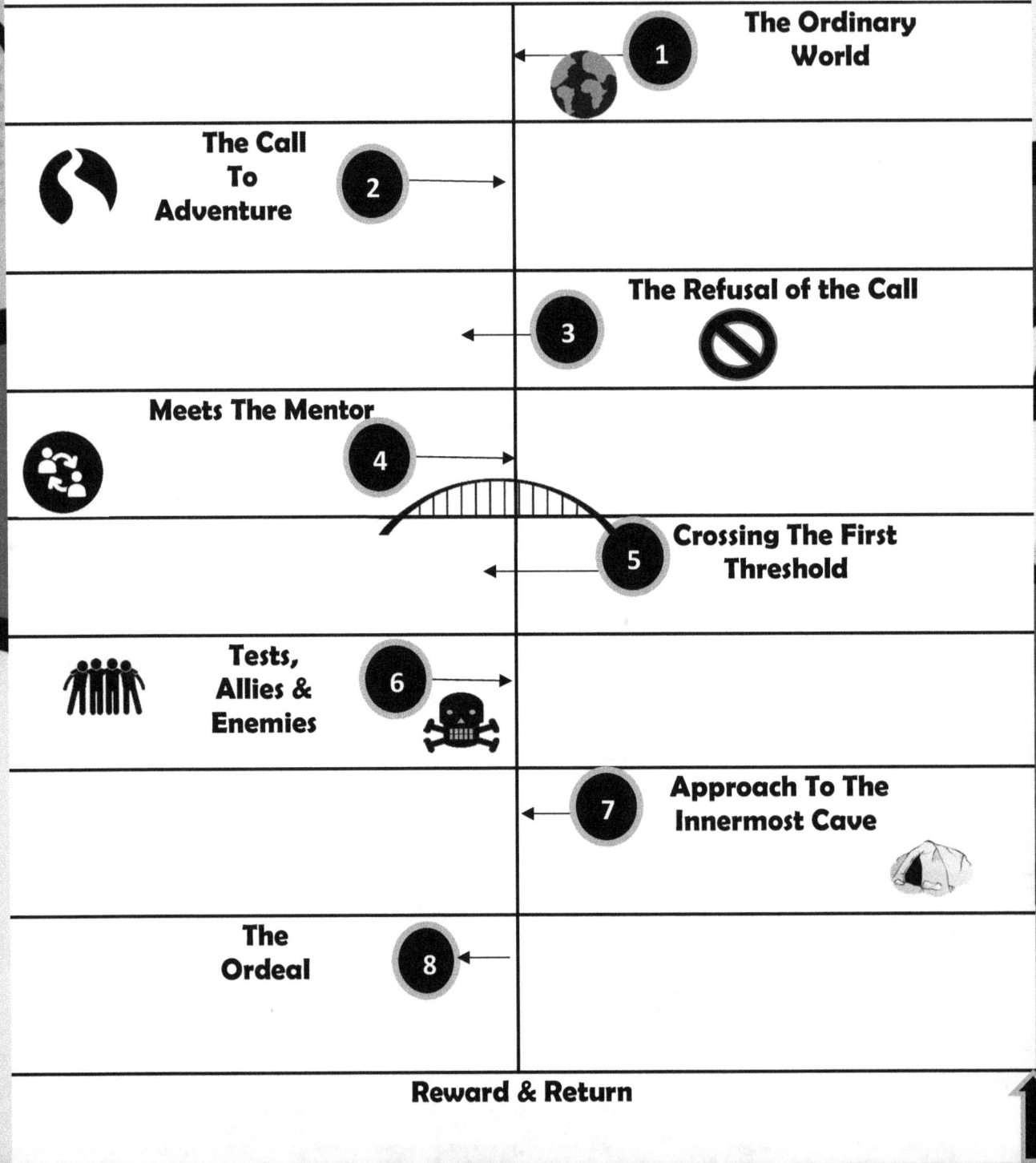

	1 — **The Ordinary World**
The Call To Adventure — 2	
	3 — **The Refusal of the Call**
Meets The Mentor — 4	
	5 — **Crossing The First Threshold**
Tests, Allies & Enemies — 6	
	7 — **Approach To The Innermost Cave**
The Ordeal — 8	
Reward & Return	

What Do You See?
What Rewards Can You Take With You To The Next Year?

" BECOMING

We are all somewhere between our lowest possibility & highest actuality.

With every transition or milestone in life, you, Rising Purpose Peep, are exchanging one possibility for another.

With every transition or milestone in life, you, Rising Purpose Peep, are moving towards your greatest impact through your type of SUPER. "

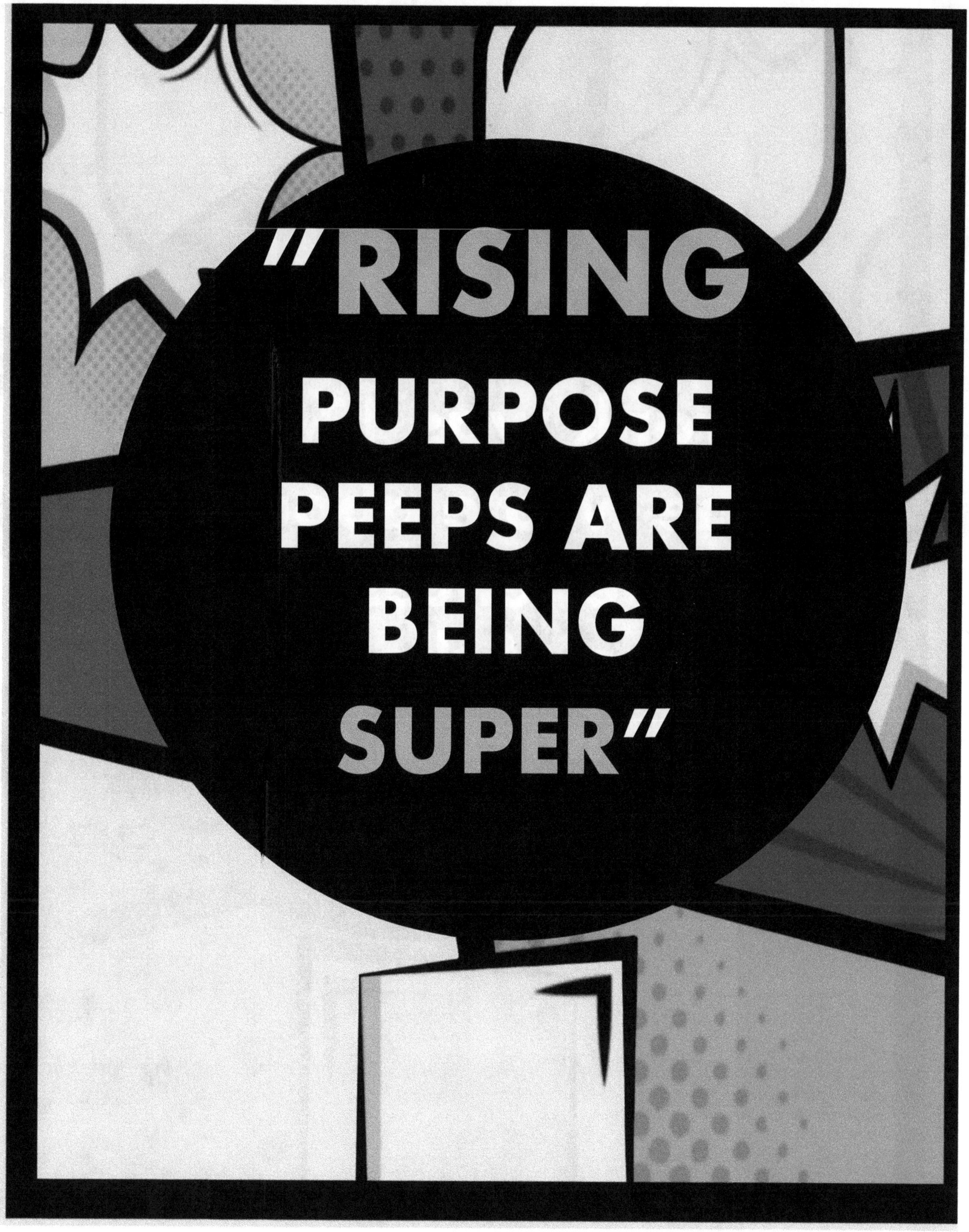
"RISING PURPOSE PEEPS ARE BEING SUPER"

"ANNE Frank was 13 when she wrote about her experiences during one of the worst times in our history."

"GRETA

Thunberg was 15 when she began protesting at the Swedish Parliament for climate change. She discovered she is super at social activism when she sparked high school students to participate in protests throughout the world."

"HANNAH & CHARLIE

LUCAS are siblings and were 15 and 12, respectively, when they developed Not OK App to prevent teen suicide. The app sends the GPS location and text to up to 5 preselected contacts. Hannah got the idea after overcoming a bout of depression after being diagnosed with an illness that causes frequent fainting. Charlie says, "he developed the app because peer support makes a difference. It's different when you hear I need help from someone you know closely."

Parade.com

"OLLIE

FORSYTH went .from not fitting in and being bullied because of being dyslexic to becoming an entrepreneur for the first time at age 13—three years younger than when his mentor, Sir Richard Branson, who also is dyslexic, became an entrepreneur. Ollie's first business was Ollie's Shop, which sold trendy jewelry. Ollie's advice is that things happen in life, but you've got to crack on with life. Onward & Upward! "

Entrepreneur.com

CALEB

MADDIX became an entrepreneur & best-selling author of *Keys To Kids Success*, & motivational speaker. How? His father is also a motivational speaker & after his parents separated, Caleb was on the road with his father. At age 6, his father challenged him to read adult motivational books. Things clicked for Caleb when he realized he had a kid version of applying this wisdom to motivate younger Purpose Peeps like you.

What Elements of the Hero's / Heroine's Journey Do You Hear In These Stories?

List How Each Purpose Peep Became His Or Her Version of Super to Connect With Extraordinary Experiences

BEING YOUR

TYPE OF SUPER involves more than being good at something, or really loving something, **or taking a stand for** something, or helping someone else with what you know and experienced, or getting rewarded or acknowledged for your contribution. **IKIGAI a combination of these things just like the Hero's & Heroine's Journey has all these things. IKIGAI (sounds like Icky Guy) is a way to pull together all your parts of being SUPER & it's fun to say.**

"

IKIGAI

is thousands of years old from two Japanese words translated to valuable living. The Purpose Peeps who practice combining four ways of being with the way they are super call it their reason for being. Think of a Venn Diagram with 4 Circles and in the center of the four circles is IKIGAI. What if when we are out of balance with one area of IKIGAI, then a call to adventure begins to help us to see it—it's usually not obvious. Followed by all the situations, events and people that guide and push us to change, *if we accept the call.*

"

"SOMETHING
interesting happens when we combine The Hero's or Heroine's Journey with IKIGAI! By using the steps of the Hero's or Heroine's Journey to answer IKIGAI type questions, the super emerges. Sometimes your super is right in front of you but you don't recognize it or say things like, "That's just the way I am," or "Doesn't everyone do that?" or "Doesn't everyone think, feel or respond like that?"

"

Although our journeys differ,

we are all filling in the answers to what we love and will stand for,

what our gifts and talents are,

what the world needs from us

& how we are grounded through recognition &reward for our contributions.

"

IKIGAI Questions

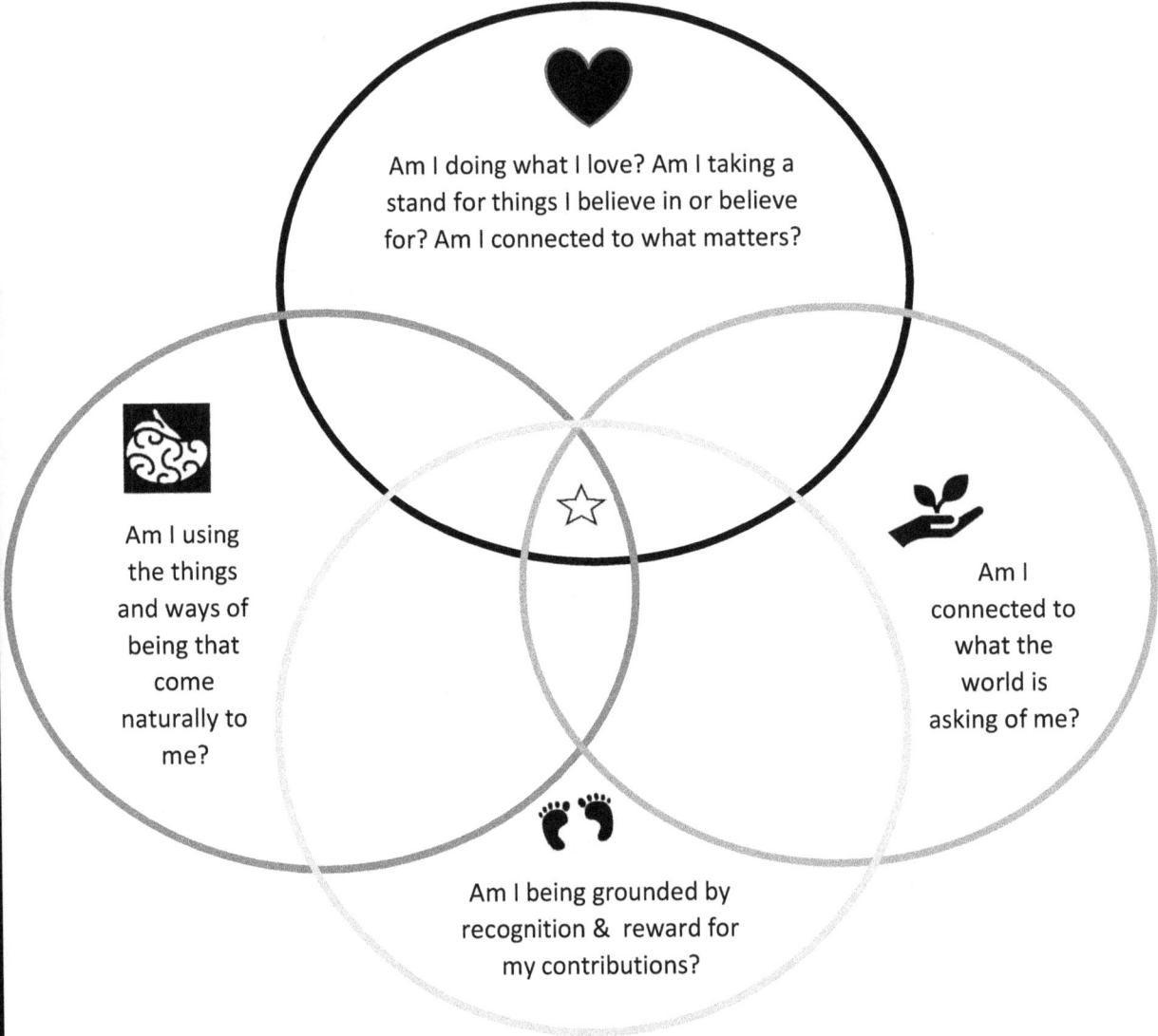

Am I doing what I love? Am I taking a stand for things I believe in or believe for? Am I connected to what matters?

Am I using the things and ways of being that come naturally to me?

Am I connected to what the world is asking of me?

Am I being grounded by recognition & reward for my contributions?

Examples of IKIGAI

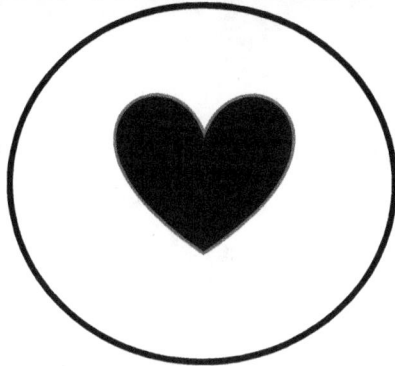

What You Love:

- Being (kind, courageous, generous, adventurous, creative, structured, scientific, innovative, compassionate, cooperative, active, healthy, balanced, expressive, reserved, unique, authentic, etc.)
- Being With (any noun including type of person or group, thoughts, experiences)
- Doing (any verb) Most people start here but it's last on purpose!

Gifts & Talents Are You Wired With:

- What do you do really well without really having to put a lot of thought into it?
- What are you doing when you completely lose track of time?
- What do you have that you generously share with others?
- What gifts have you received on your journey that you can take back to others?

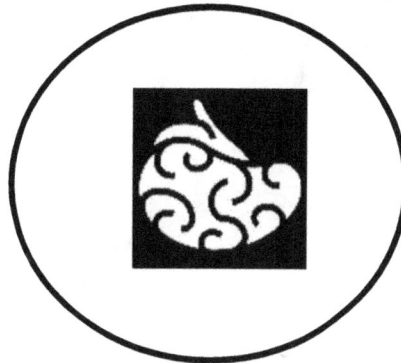

Your Ordinary World Is Asking For:

- Qualities you posses
- Unique value you bring
- Innovation from your gifts/talents/experiences
- Solutions from your gifts/talents/experiences
- Wisdom from gifts/talents/experiences

You Are Grounded Through Recognition & Reward:

- You are fulfilled in what you do
- You grow in character, wisdom & skillset
- Opportunities/Synchronicity appear
- Solutions from your gifts/talents/experiences
- You are compensated for what you do
- You are a valued member of a tribe

IKIGAI
The Wizard of Oz Example

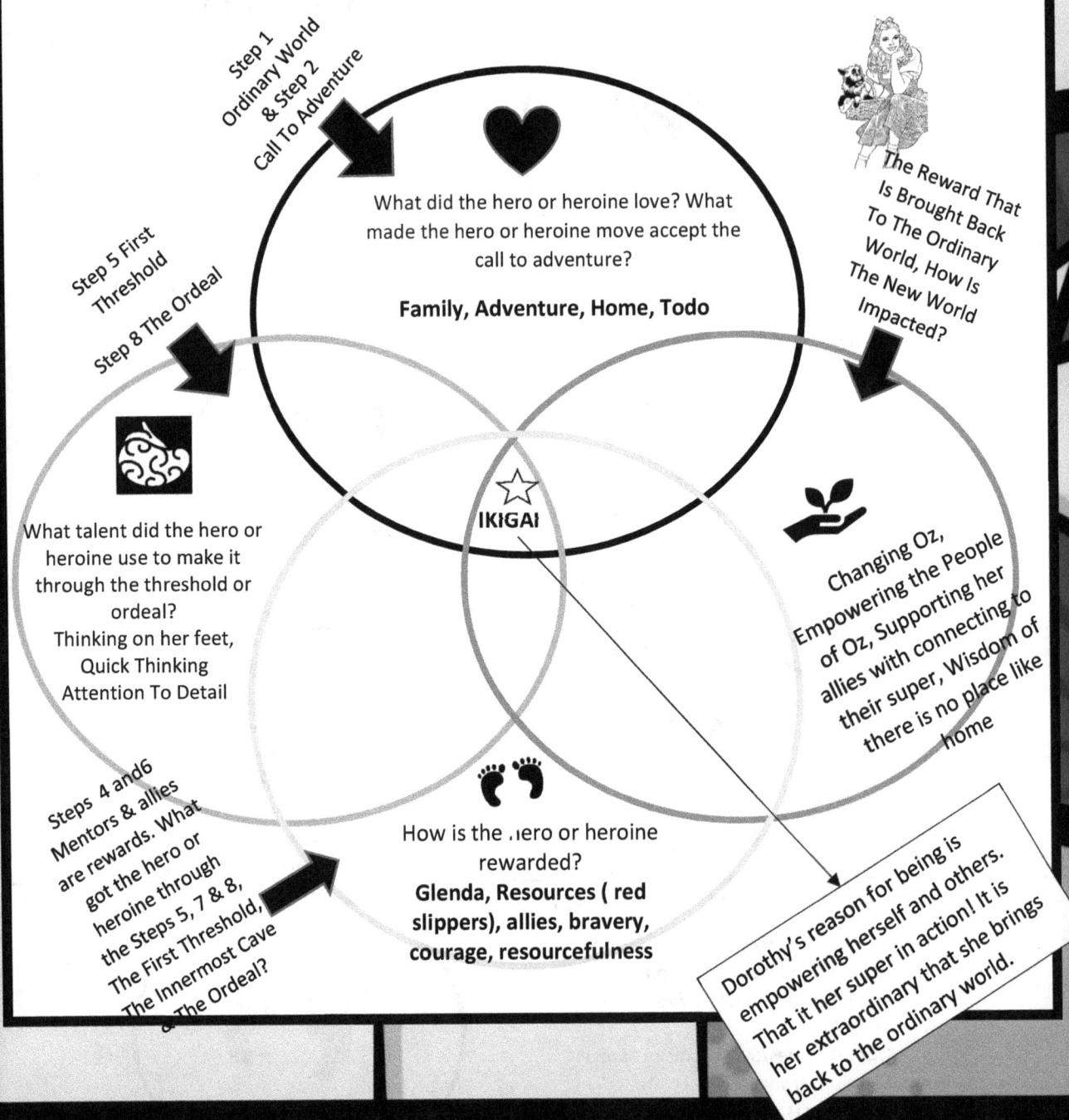

Step 1 Ordinary World & Step 2 Call To Adventure

What did the hero or heroine love? What made the hero or heroine move accept the call to adventure?

Family, Adventure, Home, Todo

The Reward That Is Brought Back To The Ordinary World, How Is The New World Impacted?

Step 5 First Threshold

Step 8 The Ordeal

What talent did the hero or heroine use to make it through the threshold or ordeal?
Thinking on her feet, Quick Thinking Attention To Detail

☆ IKIGAI

Changing Oz, Empowering the People of Oz, Supporting her allies with connecting to their super, Wisdom of there is no place like home

Steps 4 and 6 Mentors & allies are rewards. What got the hero or heroine through the Steps 5, 7 & 8, The First Threshold, The Innermost Cave & The Ordeal?

How is the hero or heroine rewarded?
Glenda, Resources (red slippers), allies, bravery, courage, resourcefulness

Dorothy's reason for being is empowering herself and others. That it her super in action! It is her extraordinary that she brings back to the ordinary world.

When You Apply IKIGAI To The Story, What Do You See?

IKIGAI
Complete Using The Harry Potter Movie

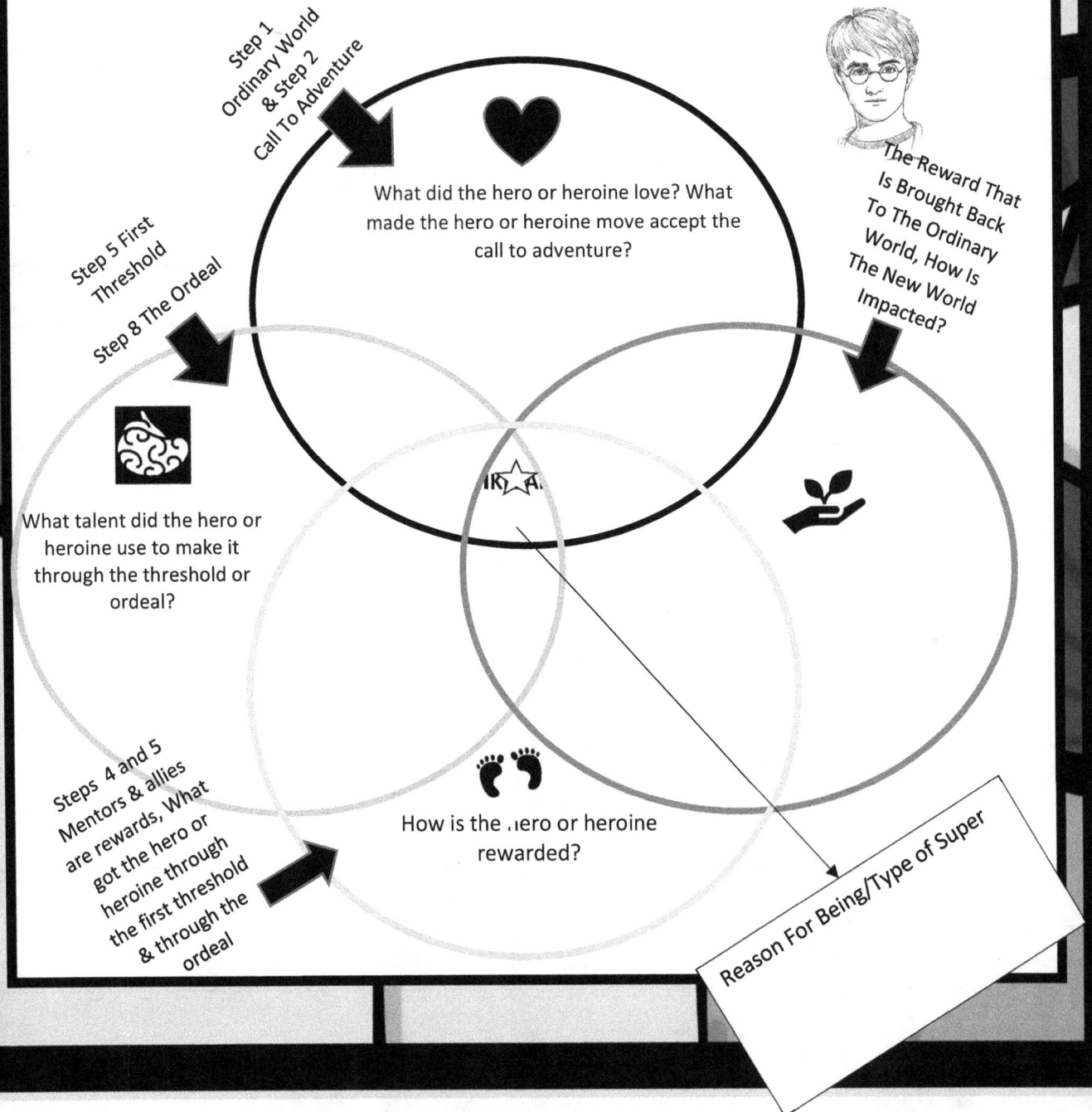

Step 1
Ordinary World
& Step 2
Call To Adventure

What did the hero or heroine love? What made the hero or heroine move accept the call to adventure?

Step 5 First Threshold

Step 8 The Ordeal

The Reward That Is Brought Back To The Ordinary World, How Is The New World Impacted?

What talent did the hero or heroine use to make it through the threshold or ordeal?

Steps 4 and 5 Mentors & allies are rewards, What got the hero or heroine through the first threshold & through the ordeal

How is the hero or heroine rewarded?

Reason For Being/Type of Super

When You Apply IKIGAI To The Story, What Do You See?

IKIGAI
Complete Using The Black Panther Movie

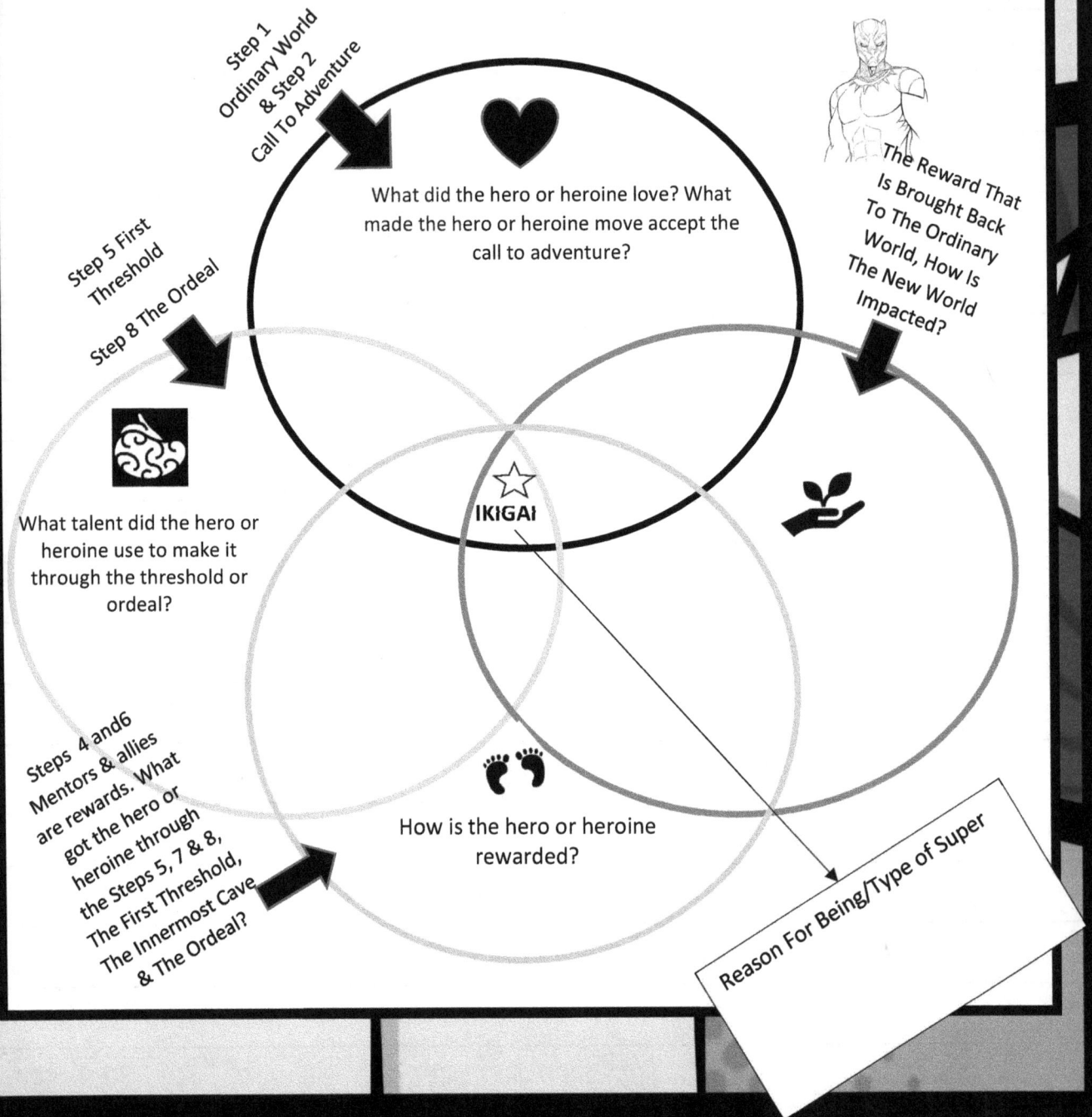

Step 1
Ordinary World
& Step 2
Call To Adventure

The Reward That
Is Brought Back
To The Ordinary
World, How Is
The New World
Impacted?

What did the hero or heroine love? What made the hero or heroine move accept the call to adventure?

Step 5 First
Threshold

Step 8 The Ordeal

What talent did the hero or heroine use to make it through the threshold or ordeal?

IKIGAI

Steps 4 and 6
Mentors & allies
are rewards. What
got the hero or
heroine through
the Steps 5, 7 & 8,
The First Threshold,
The Innermost Cave
& The Ordeal?

How is the hero or heroine rewarded?

Reason For Being/Type of Super

When You Apply IKIGAI To The Story, What Do You See?

IKIGAI
Complete Using The Mulan Movie

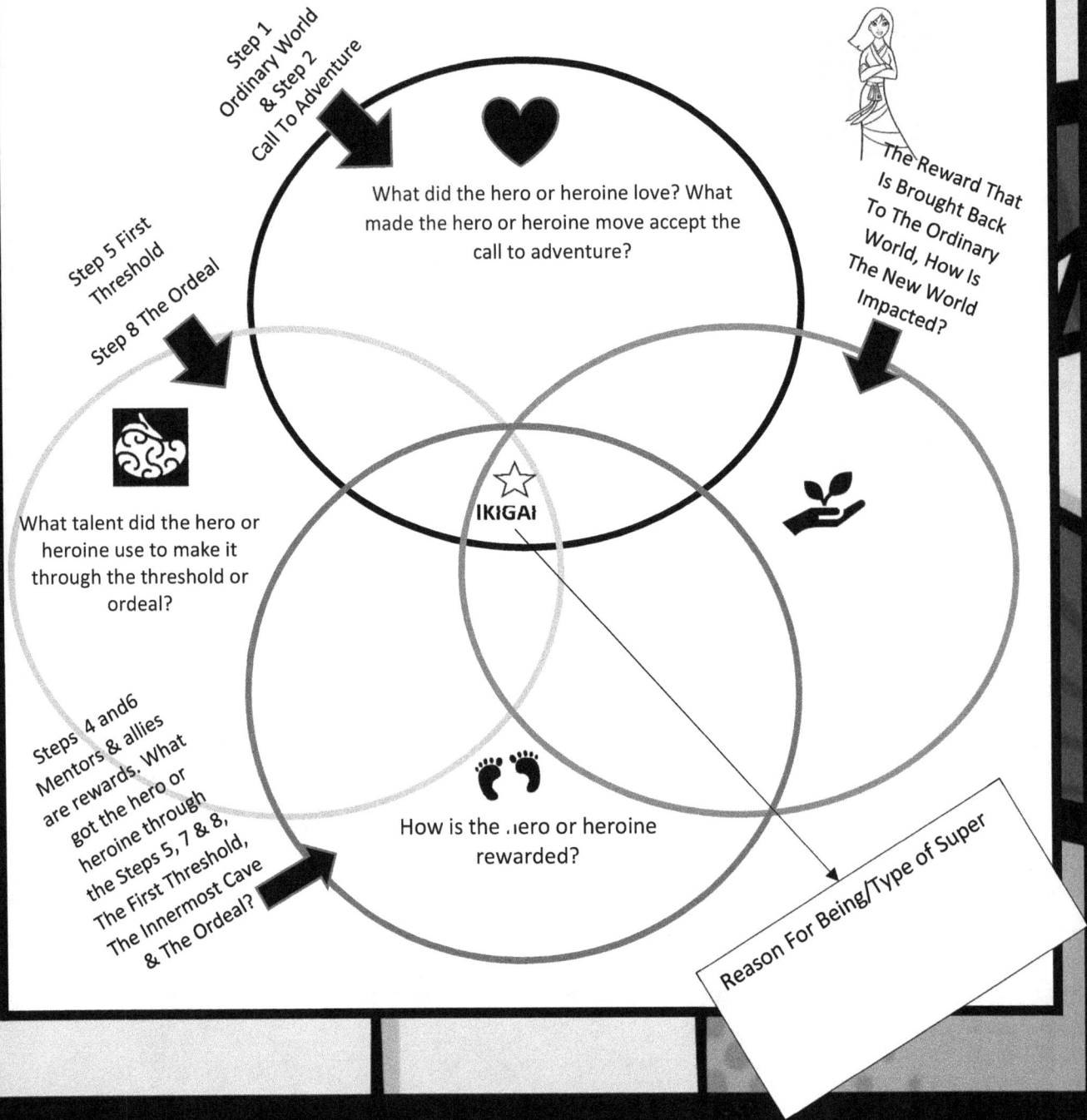

Step 1
Ordinary World
& Step 2
Call To Adventure

The Reward That
Is Brought Back
To The Ordinary
World, How Is
The New World
Impacted?

What did the hero or heroine love? What made the hero or heroine move accept the call to adventure?

Step 5 First Threshold

Step 8 The Ordeal

★ IKIGAI

What talent did the hero or heroine use to make it through the threshold or ordeal?

Steps 4 and 6
Mentors & allies
are rewards. What
got the hero or
heroine through
the Steps 5, 7 & 8,
The First Threshold,
The Innermost Cave
& The Ordeal?

How is the hero or heroine rewarded?

Reason For Being/Type of Super

When You Apply IKIGAI To The Story, What Do You See?

IKIGAI
Complete Using YOUR Story

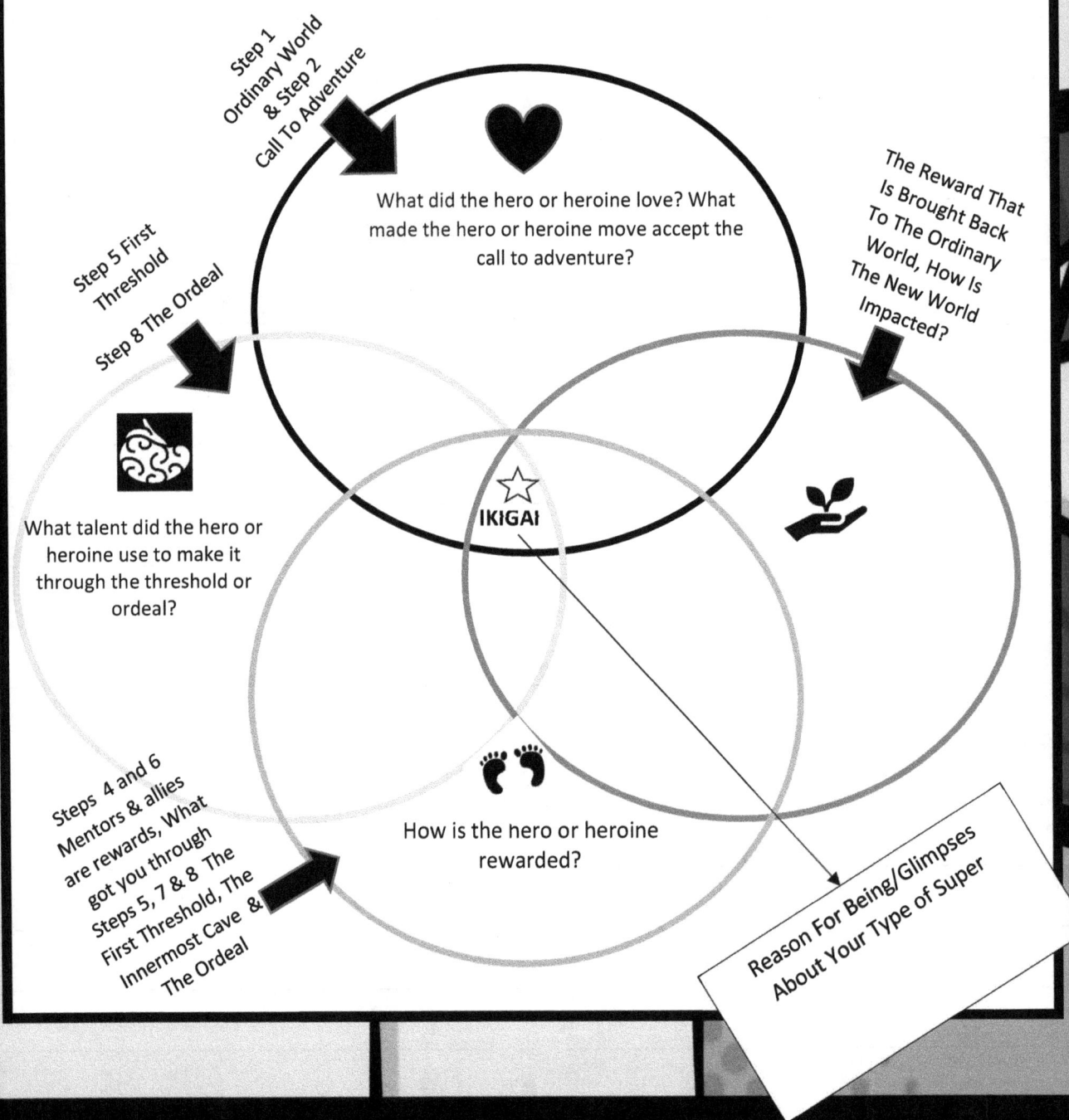

Step 1
Ordinary World
& Step 2
Call To Adventure

The Reward That
Is Brought Back
To The Ordinary
World, How Is
The New World
Impacted?

Step 5 First
Threshold

Step 8 The Ordeal

What did the hero or heroine love? What made the hero or heroine move accept the call to adventure?

What talent did the hero or heroine use to make it through the threshold or ordeal?

☆
IKIGAI

Steps 4 and 6
Mentors & allies
are rewards, What
got you through
Steps 5, 7 & 8 The
First Threshold, The
Innermost Cave &
The Ordeal

How is the hero or heroine rewarded?

Reason For Being/Glimpses About Your Type of Super

When You Apply IKIGAI To The Story, What Do You See?

How Do YOU Describe Your Reason For Being Your Type of Super

WHAT'S NEXT?

GO BE SUPER!!!!

SHARE YOUR SUPER WITH BE YOUR TYPE OF SUPER GEAR

HAVE ADVENTURES. GET TO KNOW YOUR SUPER

PRACTICE BEING SUPPORTING ROLES IN THE JOURNEY OF ANOTHER HERO'S OR HEROINE'S JOURNEY

PARTNER WITH OTHER TYPES OF SUPERS.

USE THE FOLLOWING BLANK SHEETS AFTER YOUR NEXT CALLS TO ADVENTURE TO REVIEW THE ADVENTURE...

OR WHEN YOU NEED TO REMEMBER THE HERO OR HEROINE IN YOU

The Hero's Or Heroine's Journey
of

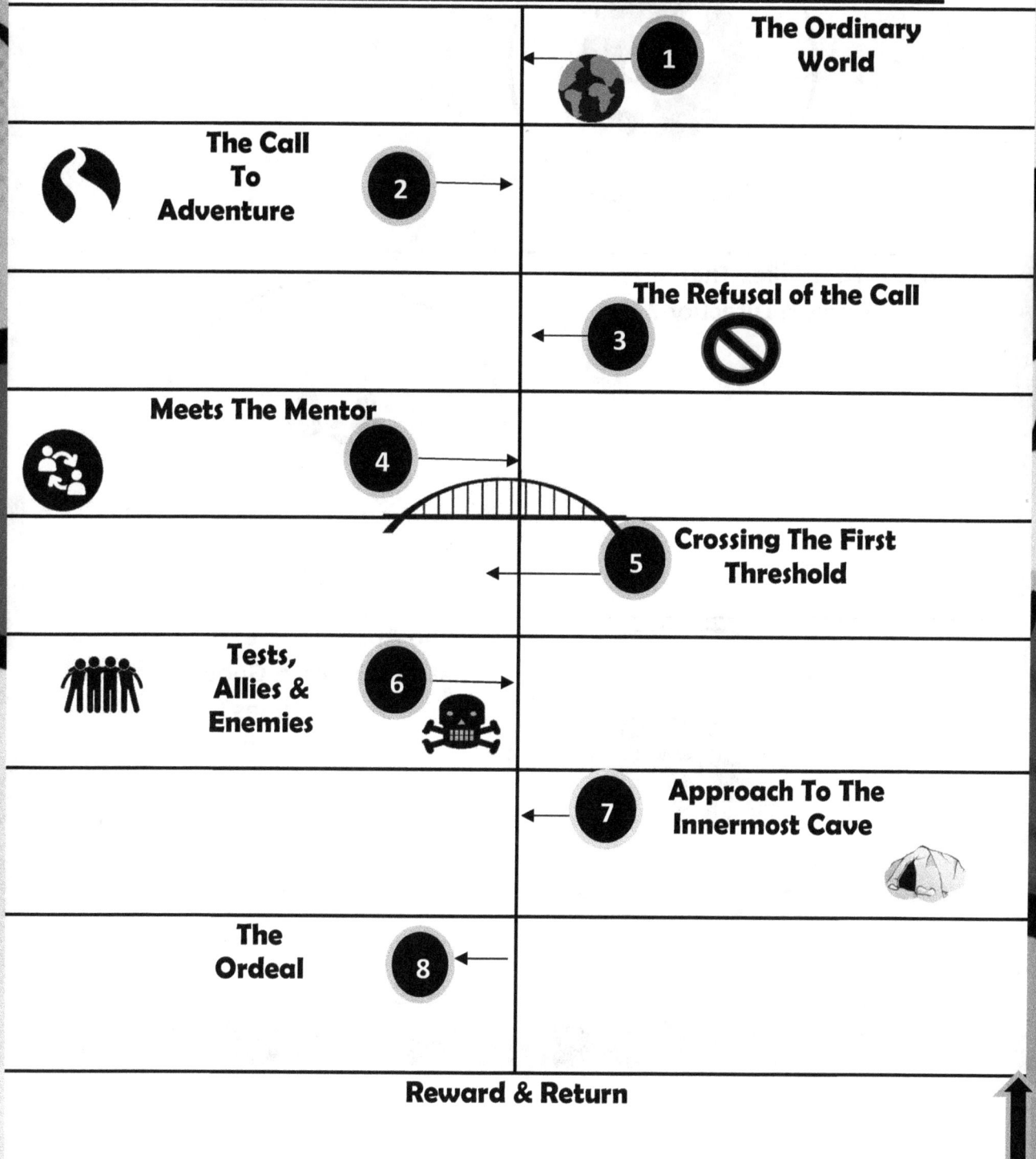

_____

	The Ordinary World 1
The Call To Adventure 2 →	
	The Refusal of the Call ← 3
Meets The Mentor 4 →	
	Crossing The First Threshold ← 5
Tests, Allies & Enemies 6 →	
	Approach To The Innermost Cave ← 7
The Ordeal 8 ←	

Reward & Return

The Hero's / Heroine's Journey
Relationship Reflection

Who Are Your Mentors That Believe You Can Do It?

Who Are Your Allies That Share Your Goals & Direction?

Who Are Your Friends, Your Tribe That Are There In Good Times & Bad Times?

The Hero's / Heroine's Journey
Impact Reflection

What Moves You Out of Your Ordinary World (Comfort Zone)?

What Are You Really Passionate About?

Who Receives The Gifts You Take Back To The Ordinary World?

The Hero's / Heroine's Journey
Growth Reflection

What Changed From The Beginning of Your Journey To Now?

What skills or knowledge are you building?

Who Supports How You Are Growing & Changing?

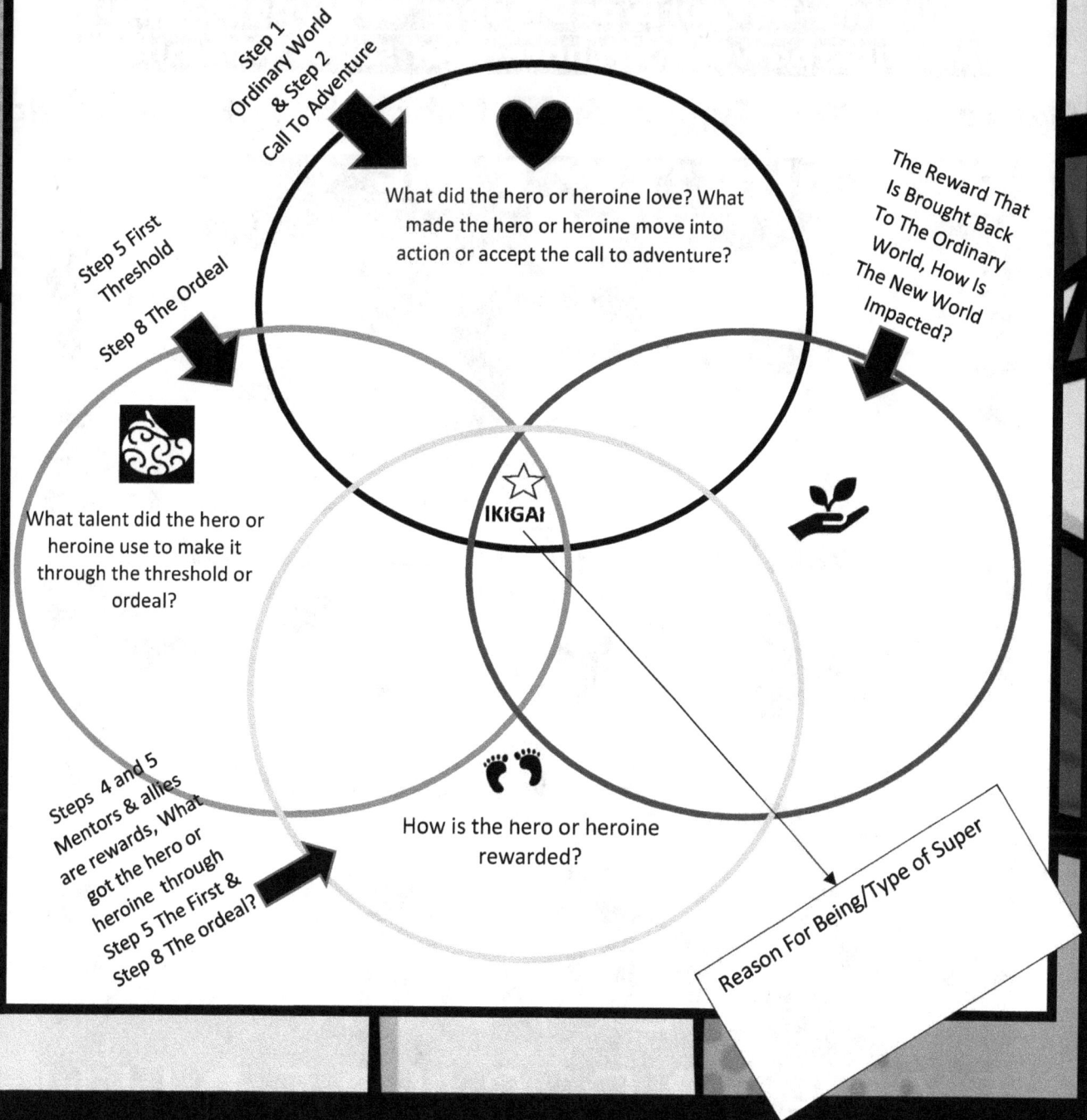

IKIGAI

Story of _____

Step 1
Ordinary World
& Step 2
Call To Adventure

The Reward That
Is Brought Back
To The Ordinary
World, How Is
The New World
Impacted?

Step 5 First
Threshold

Step 8 The Ordeal

What did the hero or heroine love? What made the hero or heroine move into action or accept the call to adventure?

What talent did the hero or heroine use to make it through the threshold or ordeal?

IKIGAI

Steps 4 and 5
Mentors & allies
are rewards, What
got the hero or
heroine through
Step 5 The First &
Step 8 The ordeal?

How is the hero or heroine rewarded?

Reason For Being/Type of Super

Visit bit.ly/Purpose Place For New Workbooks, Experiences & Gear & Be Your Type of Super Clubs & Chapters (Coming Soon)

Email questions to info@denawiggins.com

Hashtag #BeYourTypeOfSuper #MyTypeOfSuper #MySuperpowerIs to share your super with others

Get Your Be Your Type of Super Gear at bit.ly/PurposePlace